Smithsonian

LITTLE EXPLORER

AMERICAN MASTODON

by Kathryn Clay

CAPSTONE PRESS
a capstone imprint

Little Explorer is published by Capstone Press,
1710 Roe Crest Drive, North Mankato, Minnesota 56003
www.mycapstone.com

The name of the Smithsonian Institution and the sunburst
logo are registered trademarks of the Smithsonian Institution.
For more information, please visit www.si.edu.

Library of Congress Cataloging-in-Publication Data
Library of Congress Cataloging-in-Publication data is available on
the Library of Congress website.
ISBN 978-1-5435-0543-6 (library binding); ISBN 978-1-5435-0547-4
(paperback); ISBN 978-1-5435-0551-1 (eBook PDF)

Editorial Credits
Michelle Hasselius, editor; Heidi Thompson, designer;
Eric Gohl, media researcher; Kathy McColley, production specialist

Our very special thanks to Matthew T. Miller, Paleontologist
in the Department of Paleobiology at the National Museum of
Natural History, Smithsonian Institution, for his review. Capstone
would also like to thank Kealy Gordon, Product Development
Manager, and the following at Smithsonian Enterprises:
Ellen Nanney, Licensing Manager; Brigid Ferraro, Vice President,
Education and Consumer Products; Carol LeBlanc, Senior Vice
President, Education and Consumer Products; and Christopher
A. Liedel, President.

Image Credits
Alamy: National Geographic Creative, 9; Bridgeman Images: Peale
Museum, Philadelphia, PA, USA/Peale, Charles Willson (1741-1827),
27, Wood Ronsaville Harlin, Inc. USA/Private Collection/Harlin,
Greg (b.1957), 24–25; Capstone: Jon Hughes, cover, 1, 2–3, 4–5, 6–7,
10, 12–13, 22–23; iStockphoto: Aunt_Spray, 20–21; Newscom: ZUMA
Press/Hans Gutknecht, 28–29; Science Source: Kent and Donna
Dannen, 16–17, Laurie O'Keefe, 14–15; Shutterstock: Alizada Studios,
11 (top), Brooke Crigger, 5 (inset), Catmando, 22, Everett-Art, 11
(bottom), Liderina, 13 (inset), OrdinaryJoe, 30–31

Printed and bound in Canada.
010814S8

TABLE OF CONTENTS

name: American mastodon

how to say it: uh-MER-ih-kuhn MAS-toh-don

when it lived: Miocene to Pleistocene Epochs, Cenozoic Era

what it ate: plants

size: 15 feet (4.6 meters) long
7 to 10 feet (2 to 3 m) tall
weighed up to 6 tons
(5.4 metric tons)

Imagine what the world was like 20,000 years ago. There were no cars on paved roads or buildings along the horizon. Giant prehistoric animals roamed the land. This is what Earth looked like when American mastodons were alive.

Thanks to FOSSILS

A fossil is evidence of life from the geologic past. Fossil bones, teeth, hair, and tracks found in the earth have taught us everything we know about American mastodons.

ANCIENT ELEPHANTS?

American mastodons belonged to a group of animals called Proboscideans. Proboscideans have long trunks and tusks. This group includes woolly mammoths and modern elephants.

Early scientists thought American mastodon bones belonged to elephants. Others were certain these animals were deadly carnivores because of their large size. Today scientists know American mastodons ate grass and shrubs. Mastodons are only distantly related to today's elephants.

coarse hair

short tail

floppy ears

long, flexible trunk

thick tusks

columnlike legs

wide toes

MISTAKEN FOR A MAMMOTH

It can be hard to tell the difference between American mastodons and mammoths. Their body shapes are similar. Both animals were covered in thick hair and had long tusks. They also lived around the same time.

But the American mastodon is a different species. Its teeth were shaped like a series of cones. The mammoth had flat teeth. The American mastodon also had shorter tusks than the mammoth.

imperial mammoth

American mastodon

9

MIGHTY MOLARS

The American mastodon had large teeth. Each tooth was a little larger than an adult human's fist. The teeth had deep ridges that helped the animal mash up leaves, twigs, and grass.

American mastodons were herbivores. This means they ate plants.

Molars from a mastodon are on display at the Thomas Condon Paleontology Center in Oregon and many other museums around the world.

In 1772 a trader named Dr. John Connolly mailed a mastodon tooth to George Washington. Connolly had found the tooth while exploring Big Bone Lick in Kentucky. Washington kept the tooth for the rest of his life.

a painting of George Washington

TOUGH TUSKS

The American mastodon's tusks were up to 10 feet (3 m) long and bent slightly upward. American mastodons used their tusks to break off branches and eat leaves. They could also use their tusks to fight off predators and move snow to eat the grass underneath.

Scientists can learn more about an American mastodon by studying its tusks. The animal's tusks grew thicker every season. Scientists can measure the tusks' thickness to find out the time of year that the animal died. Scientists can also learn how old the animal was by studying the condition of its tusks.

One tusk was often more worn down than the other. Scientists believe this means that the American mastodon used one tusk more often. This is similar to humans, who are usually left- or right-handed.

LAYERS OF HAIR

Unlike modern elephants, American mastodons had layers of hair. The hair covered everything from the tops of their skulls to the ends of their tails.

The animal's hair grew up to 35 inches (89 centimeters) long. It kept the American mastodon warm in cold weather.

"These [fossil] animals ... differ from elephants as much as, or more than, a dog differs from the jackal and the hyena."
— scientist Georges Cuvier

FOLLOWING THE FOOTPRINTS

Because of their size, American mastodons left large footprints wherever they went. Scientists have studied these footprints and learned that these animals lived in woodlands and forests. The animal's tracks have also been found in valleys near swamps and ponds.

Scientists believe American mastodons traveled long distances in search of food, like today's elephants.

Animal footprints are called trace fossils. Trace fossils also include animal nests, burrows, and even fossilized poop!

PLEISTOCENE HOME

From Canada to Mexico, American mastodons lived throughout North America. A large number of the animal's fossils have been found south of the Great Lakes and in the eastern part of the United States.

Other Miocene and Pleistocene Animals

dire wolf

saber-toothed cat

short-faced bear

early human

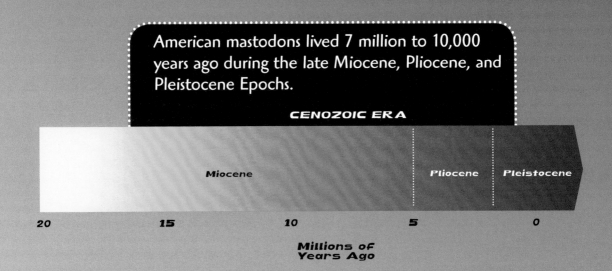

American mastodons lived 7 million to 10,000 years ago during the late Miocene, Pliocene, and Pleistocene Epochs.

CENOZOIC ERA

Miocene

Pliocene

Pleistocene

20   15   10   5   0

Millions of
Years Ago

This area and other parts of the world began to cool during the Pleistocene Epoch. This epoch is also known as the last Ice Age. During the Ice Age, many plants and animals died out because of the colder temperatures.

Other types of mastodons lived on every continent except Antarctica and Australia. A smaller species of mastodon lived in what is now Siberia.

STRONGER TOGETHER

By studying fossil sites, scientists have determined that American mastodons lived together in herds. The herds usually included females and young males. Adult males preferred to live alone.

Living in herds had many benefits. Females could help one another look after young. Living in groups also meant more animals could watch out for deadly predators.

American mastodons could live up to 60 years.

A SABER-TOOTHED SUPPER

Adult American mastodons had few predators because of their large size. But hungry meat-eaters would attack young mastodons that separated from their herds.

Saber-toothed cats used their razor-sharp claws and teeth to attack the younger mastodons. When hunting as a group, these large cats could also take down an adult American mastodon.

short-faced bear

Other predators included dire wolves, short-faced bears, and American lions.

EARLY HUNTERS

Early humans were also predators of American mastodons. Humans used the animal's bones to make weapons, musical instruments, and even homes. The animal's skin was used as clothing and to cover shelters.

In 1977 scientists found an American mastodon fossil in Washington. The fossil had a spear point stuck in its ribs. The spear was more than 13,000 years old. This proved that early humans hunted the giant animal.

FIRST FOSSIL DISCOVERIES

In 1705 a Dutch farmer found the first American mastodon tooth in Claverack, New York. The tooth weighed 5 pounds (2.3 kilograms). The farmer gave the tooth to a local politician in exchange for a glass of rum. The politician gave the tooth to the governor, who shipped the tooth to England with the label "Tooth of a Giant."

The first major American mastodon excavation took place more than 100 years later. The fossils were dug from the Big Bone Lick site in Kentucky. Scientists think the animals came to drink the water. They got stuck in the mud and eventually died.

a painting of a mastodon excavation from 1806

AMERICAN MASTODONS ON DISPLAY

Hundreds of American mastodon fossils have been found over the years. Their bones are on display in museums across North America. Studying the bones of ancient animals helps us learn what our world was like millions of years ago.

The Warren Mastodon

The American Museum of Natural History in New York City is home to the Warren Mastodon. Found in 1845, this is the first complete skeleton discovered in the United States. Today it is still one of the most complete American mastodon skeletons ever found.

a mastodon at the Natural History Museum in Los Angeles, California

GLOSSARY

ancient—from a long time ago

burrow—a tunnel or hole in the ground made or used by an animal

epoch—an amount of time that is less than a geologic period and greater than a geologic age

excavation—the process of digging into the earth to search for fossils

fossil—evidence of life from the geologic past

herd—a group of animals that lives or moves together

Miocene Epoch—the period of time beginning 23 million years ago and ending 5 million years ago

Pleistocene Epoch—the period of time beginning 2 million years ago and ending 10,000 years ago

predator—an animal that hunts another animal for food

prehistoric—living or occurring before people began to write history

Proboscidean—a group of large animals made up of elephants and extinct related species

spear—a weapon with a long handle and a pointed blade

species—a group of animals that can be interbred to produce fertile offspring

trace fossils—any proof of past life found in rocks that is not part of an animal's body

woodland—land that is covered by trees and shrubs

CRITICAL THINKING QUESTIONS

1. American mastodons are Proboscideans. Name two other animals that belong to this group.

2. American mastodons are commonly mistaken for mammoths. Describe how the animals are similar. How are they different?

3. The Warren Mastodon is displayed at the American History Museum in New York City. What makes this mastodon so unique?

READ MORE

Medina, Nico. *What Was the Ice Age?* What Was? New York: Penguin Workshop, 2017.

Zeiger, Jennifer. *Mammoth and Mastodon.* 21st Century Junior Library. Ann Arbor, Mich.: Cherry Lake Publishing, 2016.

Zoehfeld, Kathleen Weidner. *Prehistoric Mammals.* Washington, D.C.: National Geographic Children's Books, 2015.

INTERNET SITES

Use FactHound to find Internet sites related to this book.

Visit *www.facthound.com*

Just type in 9781543505436 and go.

Check out projects, games and lots more at
www.capstonekids.com

Super-cool stuff!

INDEX